The Appalachian Trail: The History of America's Longest Hiking Trail

By Charles River Editors

The Appalachian Trail's logo

Introduction

Daniel Case's picture of part of the trail

A sizeable body of literature is available on the east-west pathways of the American continent, including the famous wagon train trails that helped to colonize the nation to the shores of the Pacific. Any study of these routes ranging from footpaths to early American highways is accompanied by an equally vibrant collection of popular literature. In the perception of the American history buff, the continent was fully peopled by the advent of the 20th century, and the American mystique began to shrink with the absence of unexplored land.

However, those enamored of the primeval American experience can find comfort in a system of north-south trails designed to recapture the natural wonders of the continent, and to provide an escape from commercialism and the inherent noise of the city. The Pacific Crest Trail travels in one form or another from Canada to Mexico, while the Continental Divide Trail lies nearer the center of the county, following some of the highest points of the Rocky Mountains.

Most iconic of the major American pathways is the Appalachian Trail that completes the "triple crown"[1] of the national hiking experience. Covering a range from central Maine to Georgia at a distance of 2,193 miles, it is the longest of the three, following the crest of the Alleghenies and Blue Ridge Mountains through 14 states. All in all, it encompasses 465,000 feet in elevation and hosts three million visitors each year for at least a part of the total distance. On an annual basis, approximately 4,000 hikers begin a south to north trek beginning at Springer Mountain, Georgia, with the goal of hiking all the way to Maine. The northerly direction is greatly

---

[1] Michael Lanza, Backpacker, Outside, July 4, 2021 – www.backpacker.com/trips/long-trails/appalachian-trail/american-classic-hiking-the-appalachian-trail/

preferred, in part because of the weather calendar and because the northern terminus closes in mid-October, creating a difficulty for slow travelers.

The Origins of the Trail

The evolution of one of the East's most distinct cultural
emblems was first conceived in 1921 and acted upon
officially four years later. The earliest segments of the
trail were built by private citizens representing local and
state "trail clubs," but the entire length was completed in a
period of 12 years with the eventual participation of the
National Park Service, the U.S. Forest Service, the
Appalachian Trail Conservancy, numerous state agencies,
and thousands of volunteers.

The original trail was the brainchild of Benton MacKaye,
a forester and philosopher from Massachusetts. He had
attended Harvard University in the early years of the 20th
century and at that time envisioned a long interstate
walking path before joining the fledgling U.S. Forest
Service. MacKaye came to interpret the American social
landscape as two conflicting cultures, the "metropolitan
and the indigenous."[2] On the increasingly dominant side
was industry and commerce marked by inhumane cities
filled with "brutalizing slums"[3] and the accompanying
"cancerous tissue"[4] of suburban growth. Metropolitanism,
in MacKaye's view, was the cause of many non-urban
problems due to the "improvident"[5] use of natural

[2] Ronald Foresta, Transformation of the Appalachian Trail, *Geographical Review*, Vol. 77 No. 1 (January, 1987)

[3] Ronald Foresta

[4] Ronald Foresta

[5] Ronald Foresta

resources and the "destabilization"[6] of traditional society, in this case rural society. MacKaye loved what he called the "indigenous life,"[7] to which he referred as "the pervasive source of man's true living."[8]

MacKaye

This traditional American way of life began to erode, according to MacKaye, around the time of the Civil War. The primary signs of what he saw as decay included the network of railroads crisscrossing the east, and the advent

---

[6] Ronald Foresta

[7] Ronald Foresta

[8] Ronald Foresta

of motorized transport and electric power. He advocated public ownership of all natural resources and devised various strategies for the use of public lands, especially timber and mineral-laden areas. This, he felt, would rejuvenate the antebellum American culture, rebalancing the coexistence with commerce and industry.

MacKaye transferred to the Department of Labor and concentrated on a regimen of community planning. A long footpath was only part of his scheme. He proposed a network of logging communities throughout the nation's forests and put out a call to academics for "reinvestigating the nation's spirit."[9] His general vision first appeared in the essay *Appalachian Trail: A Project in Regional Planning*, published in the Journal of American Architecture, in which he sought to arouse interest in returning the American countryside to a place of "refuge."[10] As for the proposed trail, MacKaye believed that "for all practical purposes, [it] should be endless…the backbone of a primeval environment."[11]

The first tangible signs of manifesting such a prodigious trail occurred when MacKaye convened a conference in Washington, D.C. in 1922. This meeting spurred a wave of interest in several states along the proposed route. The

---

[9] John C. Inescoe, University of Georgia, Appalachian Trail, New Georgia Encyclopedia, 10/02/2002 – www. Georgiaencyclopedia..

org/articles/sports-outdoor-recreation/Appalachian-trail

[10] John C. Inescoe

[11] John C. Inescoe

first section was built in New York in 1922, with a proposed segment along the southern terminus of Lookout Mountain, straddling the border between Georgia and Tennessee.

The conference was the first occasion in which people active in promoting each aspect of the proposed trail met together. It was so successful that it almost immediately melded into one permanent group, with W.A. Welch as Chairman, Harlean James as Secretary, and Benton MacKaye as Field Secretary. Topographically, the trail was designed to run "through each of the highland regions"[12] of every state.

At the time, Tennessee, Pennsylvania, and Virginia were locations in which marked trails were rare. With the understanding that few would ever conquer the entire distance, accessibility from every city was made a priority. However, south of Palisades Park in New York, the only open ground available was in the recently constructed and designated national forests, which immediately brought about the involvement of the federal government.

Conceived as "the backbone of a super reservation and primeval recreation ground"[13] covering the length and

[12] Benton MacKaye, The Appalachian Trail: A Guide to the Study of Nature, The Scientific Monthly, Vol. 34 No. 4 (April, 1932

[13] Benton MacKaye

width of the Appalachian Range in terms of used land and accessibility, topographical realities had to be taken into account. The Appalachian Range has reached its present state in two geological "generations," the "Older" and "Newer." The "Older" bedrock forms a chain from the Great Smoky Mountains of Tennessee to the White Mountains in the north, and this chain is only broken in one place, near the Susquehanna River in Pennsylvania. The "Newer" Appalachia is embodied within the Allegheny Mountains, "a sort of magnified ploughed playground"[14] that flanks the "Older" on the west side. Between the older and the newer strata lies a corridor known as the "Great Valley" that runs from Chattanooga to Lake Champlain. East and west of the twin ranges is a symmetric pattern of plain and plateau.

East of the "Older" portion lies southern Piedmont and the New England Upland, ancient crystalline areas. West of the "Newer" strata lies the middle-aged Allegheny plateau. East of Piedmont spreads the Atlantic coastal plain, newly emerged from the ocean.

The Appalachian Trail follows the crest of the "Older" portion with the exception of its arrival at the Susquehanna. There, it crosses to the "Newer" over the "Great Valley." The "Old" portion is all ancient underlying hard crystalline material. Of the younger,

---

[14] Benton MacKaye

uncrystallized softer material includes sandstone and shale. One has been exposed for much longer than the other, dividing the land into flat and mountainous topography.

The Blue Ridge of Virginia lies to the south, and a great deal of volcanic activity still occurs in the region, as far west as Missouri. The climatic cycle of the Appalachian's forest goes back approximately 70,000 years, so modern animal life is fairly stabilized. As to the question of how the myriad of species survives in such an environment, the answer is that they do it the same way people do: cooperation and division of labor, seasoned with the occasional "tough experience"[15] of competition.

Progress in further construction was sporadic until 1925, when a permanent Appalachian Trail Conference was established. Additional segments were sporadic, with progress in New England and Pennsylvania proceeding more rapidly than in the south. Nonetheless, the Appalachian Trail Conference was to become the most prolific organization to come out of the conference, a "simple and permanent organization."[16] MacKaye continued as Field Secretary and membership skyrocketed, "so great was the progress recorded and so firm the belief of those attending in the feasibility and

---

[15] Benton MacKaye

[16] Arthur C. Comey, The Appalachian Trail Conference, *Landscape Architecture Magazine*, Vol. 15, No. 3 (April 1925)

value of the through post trail."[17] Metropolitan dwellers from north to south were to be given access to previously untraveled regions.

Within a year, however, zest for MacKaye's idea had waned somewhat, and the quest for balance between the commercial and traditional had "degenerated into a fireside philosophy."[18] It took an energized and persistent individual to revive interest and make the trail a "vital living thing."[19] Arthur Perkins, a retired lawyer from Hartford, Connecticut, was the ideal figure for resurrecting the collective interest in the Appalachian project.

A gathering of friends and associates joined with Perkins in reviving interest and assisted with the realities of launching such a project. These included Clarence Stein, Chairman of the American Institute of Architects. Charles Whitaker, Editor of the Journal of the American Institute of Architects, joined the effort. Louis Post, who had served as the Assistant Secretary of Labor in the Woodrow Wilson administration, was also involved, as was his wife Alice, a successful reformer in her own right. Given the talents present in such a group, it nevertheless failed to provide the leadership needed to get the project off the ground. Some opine that the trail was too much of

---

[17] Arthur C. Comey

[18] Myron H. Avery, The Appalachian Trail, *Scientific American*, Vol. 153 No. 1 (July, 1935)

[19] Myron H. Avery

a part-time concern, and that the one necessary passionate individual never stepped forward.

Nonetheless, some progress was made. Over a three-year period, a logo was designed, some important organizational meetings were held, and a few new sections were built, but implementation of ideas was both "erratic and lacked coherence."[20] However, a new group was to take control, consisting of individuals who took a strong avocational interest in the outdoors, finally adding the needed momentum. Three were of particular importance. Raymond H. Torrey, an editor and columnist for the New York Post, emphasized the joys of hiking and the general outdoor life in his publication. Major William Welch, the general manager of the Palisades Interstate Park in New York, was eager to extend the love of hiking to the outer edges of New York City. Myron Avery, recruited by Perkins, was likely more responsible for the eventual success of the trail than anyone else. A Maine native and Harvard grad like MacKaye, he became a specialist in maritime law by the age of 33, residing in Washington, D.C. At that time, he had already served as the Chairman of the Appalachian Trail Conference and was known as a meticulously dressed skilled negotiator and advocate. In his early career, he spent much of his spare time exploring Mount Katahdin before it became the

---

[20] Ronald Foresta

northern terminus of the trail. In his time with the Conference, a total of over 20 years leading up to his death, Avery "tirelessly promoted, scouted and built the trail."[21] Other states soon followed suit, and many young professionals followed his example.

MacKaye and Avery

Avery was also the founder of Potomac Appalachian Trail Club, which helped numerous other mid-Atlantic clubs to emerge. His no-nonsense approach made him popular with federal agencies, especially the U.S. Forest Service. He was the first individual to ever walk the entire distance of the Appalachian Trail, one segment at a time.

Although he served such a long tenure with the Conference, Avery's greatest strengths became his greatest weaknesses due to his "demanding

[21] Ronald Foresta

nature…confrontational writing style, and unwillingness to compromise"[22] He is said to have left a "trail of broken friendships and broken personal relationships."[23]

Forging a Trail

A picture of part of the trail in South Mountain State Park, Maryland

[22] Appalachian Trail Histories, Myron Avery – www.appalachiantrailhistories.org/exhibits/builders/mavery
[23] Appalachian Trail Histories

Pete Unseth's picture of part of the trail in Pennsylvania

In 1930, the Georgia Appalachian Trail Club began working on the southern terminus, changing the trail's end to Mt. Oglethorpe near Amicola Falls, then moving it 20 miles to the present-day Springer Mountain. Actual construction of various segments was vitalized after 1933, as the Civilian Conservation Corps joined the effort. The final section of the new Appalachian Trail opened in Maine in 1937. One might predict that the various clubs and attached local organizations would precede the trail, but it turned out that at every locale, "the trail has been the pioneer."[24]

The original vision of MacKaye has become somewhat tempered through the years. The trail was to represent a "new socio-economic domain"[25] where traditional American life could be reconstructed in a "modern context,"[26] one in which "communitarian principles would order social relationships."[27] MacKaye envisioned the springing up of permanent camping communities around shelters, with their own economies based on timber, farming, or local manufacturing. It is presently difficult to imagine such first visions without incredulity, as MacKaye spoke having never witnessed mass migrations to the cities, and booming corporations that dwarfed those of his day.

However, the Appalachian Trail has taken its place among the best known "cultural element[s]"[28] of eastern

---

[24] Myron H. Avery

[25] Ronald Foresta

[26] Ronald Foresta

[27] Ronald Foresta

[28] Ronald Foresta

America, riding the summits of the Appalachian highlands. MacKaye's hope that individuals and families from eastern cities would gain "perspective on the social context of their lives"[29] through brief vacations and camping was somewhat fulfilled. Further, his efforts did address two concerns, the uncontrolled growth and the changing character of major cities, and the increasingly stagnant nature of rural America.

In what would be seen as an extreme liberal position in 21st century politics, MacKaye attempted to demonstrate that cooperatively organized communities were a more just and efficient economic model than capitalistic corporations. He believed that government-held natural resources could be employed to redirect the American economy toward a more satisfactory distribution of power and wealth. This was to be accomplished through a "homestead concept"[30] that has been recently revived in western irrigation projects. The only flaw to proving its worth was that it came too late. By the time of MacKaye's first mention of the Appalachian project, any assault on modern industrial society was already forbidden. Commercial expansion was embedded in the shrine of American success.

The Appalachian Trail Project, however, had great

----

[29] Ronald Foresta

[30] Ronald Foresta

appeal as a recreation and restoration entity to one societal group, "modern professionals whose fortunes were based on metropolitanism and industrialism MacKaye so disliked."[31] Such an interest by confirmed capitalists was to both ensure the trail's success, but to render it up as a short-term restorative regimen and emblem of the appreciation of nature. MacKaye's 'communities' were never to materialize.

Slowly, the trail filled in. Harvey Broome became the driving force behind the Smoky Mountains Hiking Club, joined by fellow Harvard-trained lawyer Frank Fowler. Much of the trail through Virginia was scouted by a professor of Ophthalmology at the University of Virginia in Charlottesville. In Pennsylvania, the two most important figures for establishing the trail were a college professor and a physician. Many federal employees were involved in the Washington-based Potomac Appalachian Trail Club. Further north in New England, Scientists, academics, and graduate students from various New England universities provided the impetus.

The Blue Eagle Climbing Club was in the beginning limited to 100 "community leaders,"[32] all men from the area. At the Dartmouth Outing Club, students and faculty from the college worked together. In contrast, the Georgia

---

[31] Ronald Foresta

[32] Ronald Foresta

Appalachian Trail Club was staffed with many young, affluent single men and women. The managers of national forests and two national parks aided in construction of large segments of the trail. State foresters in Maine, Pennsylvania and Georgia had their staffs cut many sections of trail, the latter finishing the southern terminus. Officers of the various organizations ordered departmental employees of state and federal agencies to attend staff meetings. In an effective mix of private, state, and federal workers mixed with volunteers of all stripes, the 1930 Civilian Conservation Corps was brought increasingly into the fold.

Leadership increasingly viewed the trail as a strictly recreational facility, a further departure from MacKaye's vision. Various city dwellers wrote practical books on sporting, firearms, and woodcraft, as well as "colorful descriptive ones."[33] Broome became the author of "introspective"[34] essays describing the benefits of personal contact with the American wilderness., while Avery wrote nostalgically about the natural history of his home state of Maine. Raymond Torrey authored the *New York Walk Book*, a practical trail guide and a "masterpiece of descriptive prose."[35]

All of these volumes were in one way or the other "anti-

---

[33] Ronald Foresta

[34] Ronald Foresta

[35] Ronald Foresta

modern," [36] whether romantic, philosophical, or practical, and it could be said they fall into a literary genre of "escape."[37] In addition to being recreational, the trail was now intended for a temporary respite from the rigors of metropolitan life. However, it was passionately observed by much of the leadership. A friend of Broome wrote of Avery that "The law was his means of making a living, but the wilderness was his way of life."[38] Since they were professionally secure, they virtually all failed to mention the attending social issues felt so deeply by MacKaye. The bond was now based on a "satisfaction that came from temporarily departing contemporary society."[39] Individuals who worked in the large cities "could bring equilibrium to their lives."[40]

Fortunately, however, no overriding social context set in for the trail. Progressive land managers helped to keep it that way, becoming the heirs to John Muir and John Burroughs, thought to be harmless but impractical people. MacKaye lived long enough to see his beloved trail come under federal protection, and both the transition and conflict of the trail from community-based to a recreational facility became "uncontested and forgotten."[41] It would be replaced by the "linkage of leisure activity

---

[36] Ronald Foresta

[37] Ronald Foresta

[38] Ronald Foresta

[39] Ronald Foresta

[40] Ronald Foresta

[41] Ronald Foresta

with practicality,"[42] with deep roots in the search for efficiency in American capitalism.

The trail has been treated to an ongoing regimen of renewal and vigilant care ever since. A study of the "primitive huts"[43] found along the trail offers a glimpse into a bygone era of social projects. New Deal programs that became a justification for the Civilian Conservation Corps since 1937 extensively "relocated, rebuilt, and reallocated from private to publicly owned land."[44] Today, there are 250 trail shelters over the entire trail's distance.

Despite the divergence of MacKay's way of life from the trail's eventual manifestation, a few of the original principles remain. The trail was built so that metropolitan citizens would become "acquainted with"[45] the national landscape and absorb the American scenery. The intention, however, was to have the observer "do something, not just admire something."[46] By walking through the expanse, the trail and its surrounding country was intended to exert a "primeval influence"[47] on the hiker, breathing fresh mountain air and maintaining a regimen of mental and physical exercise. Whatever the size of the trek, instead of an object doing what it was

[42] Ronald Foresta

[43] Ronald Foresta

[44] Ronald Foresta

[45] Benton MacKaye

[46] Benton MacKaye

[47] **Benton MacKaye**

built to do for the operator, hiking the trail was a process of "feeling what you touch and seeing what you look at."[48] The educational component was designed to assist the hiker to view his new landscape armed with some knowledge of its "close knit society of plants and animal life."[49] It is said that the planet's story is told in the structure of the Appalachian Range, and that the Earth's life is in its forests, a "close knit society of plants and animal life containing every race alive, save one – that one is man."[50] The trail serves to connect "rural communities, working farms and forests,"[51] squeezing through rapidly developing regions and "pro[viding] the foundation of outdoor recreation and tourism opportunities."[52]

The trail is specifically designated as a footpath, and no travel by horseback, bicycles, or motorized transport is allowed. Visitors are limited to three days within a 30-mile stretch of the trail at a single shelter. Oddly enough, hunting is permitted on the trail in sections that pass through the National Forest System, but rules specify that the entire trail is a "leave no trace" zone, and hikers and campers are urged to keep voices down and minimize the noise of electronics. They are simultaneously urged to

---

[48] Benton MacKaye

[49] Benton MacKaye

[50] Benton MacKaye

[51] Benton MacKaye

[52] Benton MacKaye

share scenic vistas and shelters and step off the trail onto durable ground when either resting or allowing others to pass.

Authority over the Appalachian Trail being divided gives more than one organization the right to set or change policy. The U.S. Forest Service is foremost among the governing bodies, able to take special actions in addition to formulating rules. In a prime example, one year after a crowd of campers left popular viewing spot Max Patch in a devastated condition, the Forest Service initiated a two-year ban on all camping. It took the full time to heal the land of the strewn garbage, human waste, and other blights. Hikers can only visit Max Patch from one hour before sunrise to one hour after sunset. Horses are prohibited, dogs and other animals are required to be on leash, and groups must be of ten individuals or fewer. Fines up to $10,000 are levied, and the area is under constant monitoring by drones. In a second instance, the Forest Service issued black bear warnings along the trail in the Nantahala and Pisgah National Forests after reports of increasing encounters. As the animals became emboldened, they took down bear bags and rifled through camping gear, bringing about a seven-mile camping ban.

The U.S. Park Service handles much of the maintenance, public education, and promotional aspects of the trail. They also issue bear warnings and spread localized information. In the Chattahoochee Range, the U.S. Park Service required all campers and hikers to employ scent-proof bear cannisters between Jarrad Gap and Neels Gap. Similarly, all hikers were urged to wear or carry some recognizable object of the color orange more easily seen at a distance.

The Appalachian Trail Conservancy, having a much older involvement with the project, is given the authority to either close parts of the trail, or shut down some of its facilities along the way. In the Covid epidemic of 2020 and 2021, the Conservancy deactivated many of the available camping shelters to avoid non-social distancing conditions. Campers were urged to use only personal tents at a greater distance apart, and to wear face coverings.

The Appalachian Trail Conservancy involves itself in many of the inevitable legal collisions between the trail and alternate use of the land. In a 2020 Supreme Court Case, the first of its kind dealing with the National Trail System Act, the question of pipelines either paralleling or falling within the 'buffer zone' of the trail came into question. In the United States Forest Service v. Cowpasture River Preservation Association, the court kept in place a policy under which thousands of volunteers, professionals, and agencies had worked for many decades.

Again in 2020, Atlantic Coast Pipeline sought to

construct a 604-mile natural gas pipeline from West Virginia to North Carolina, along a route that traversed 16 miles within the George Washington National Forest. Atlantic Coast had secured a permit from the National Forest Service for a 0.1-mile segment that came within 600 feet of the Appalachian Trail. Respondents claimed that even that short distance was a violation of the Mineral Leasing Act, maintaining that the Leasing Act did not empower the Forest Service to grant such right-of-way. The other side, however, claimed that the plan did not in any way "transform the land,"[53] and therefore the Forest Service could issue it. Congress had only spoken of right-of-way, and not "land transfers."[54] The original majority opinion was, however reversed and remanded, with Justice Sotomayor writing the dissent.

31 different clubs contribute on a regular basis, maintaining and rebuilding segments of the trail. Within these organizations are hundreds of sub-groups. Annually, over 500 volunteers from eight local trail clubs contribute more than 27,500 hours for maintenance. The full membership and availability of the full roster of clubs is much larger.

The Maine Appalachian Trail Club is the dominant force for upper New England. The trail covers a distance of 267

---

[53] Supreme Court of the United States, U.S. Forest Service v. Cowpasture River Preservation Association, Court of Appeals for the Fourth Circuit – www.supremecourt.gov/opinions/19pdf/18-1854_igdj.pdf

[54] Supreme Court of the United States

miles in the state of Maine, requiring a great deal of
maintenance. The New England region spans 734 miles,
which can be traversed in approximately 57 days. The
Maine portion of the trail is considered to be particularly
wild and "spectacularly scenic."[55] In the central
wilderness is the northern terminus for the trail, Mt.
Kitahdin, and an unofficial extension to the Appalachian
trail proceeds north into Canada, terminating in
Newfoundland and Labrador. Kitahdin stands at 5,627
feet of elevation, and the route continues through Baxter
Park, and continues across the Kennebec River before
passing through the famed Mahoosik and Grafton Notches
and going its way into New Hampshire.

The mission of the MATC has remained a constant since
1935. An active website seeks new members to join a
work trip to labor alongside specialists in trail
maintenance, help out with campsite management,
monitor corridors, and lend off-trail support.

Seven executive Directors run the MATC organization,
and the organizations features a Ridge Runner Education
Department. Three ridge runners are positioned on the
trail at all times between May and October, and encounter
at least 10,000 people each year. They are usually based at
high-use recreational destinations, including the Gulf
Hagas, 'The Grand Canyon of Maine.' Other sites are

---

generally on or around Saddleback and Bigelow Peaks, two examples of 4,000-foot peaks on the western Maine portion of the trail. They teach backcountry knowledge, skills and ethics, monitor for threats to alpine plants and wildlife habitat, and water resources. They also mitigate fire impacts, discourage rowdy behavior, littering and inappropriate waste deposits. Their subject matter is broad, from hanging a bear bag, fording a river, reading maps, digging a 'cat hole,' identifying alpine plants, to using a gray water pit.

The MATC releases annual reports, including ferry reports. By the end of 2019, the Kennebee River Ferry had brought 2,378 hikers across without injury. The MATC publishes a newsletter entitled the *Mainetainer* that includes a work trips calendar and a description of each project, and a membership recruiting page with $25 for dues.

The Path

A picture of Franconia Ridge in New Hampshire

A picture of the trail in Massachusetts

Most who take the entirety of the trail travel from south to north, going from Georgia to Maine. It is best to leave around mid-March through early April. To avoid the crowds, one can depart mid-April to the first week of May, but they must walk faster since the northern terminus of Mount Katahdin closes on October 15. Departing from Maine in a southward direction is the less comfortable choice because the hardest climbing would have to be done in the coldest weather. In the north, fickle weather should be expected, and travelers should take rest days during storms. Shelters are stationed about nine miles apart, but the White Mountains become steeper and rockier, and the daily distance will be reduced. However, if hikers fall behind, they can often make up part of the distance down the home stretch.

The terminus of the trail in Maine

  Once the trail enters New Hampshire, much of the primary care shifts to the Randolph Mountain Club. The organization manages 102 miles of trail in the state, the bulk of it on the northern slopes of Mount Madison, Mount Adams, and Mount Jefferson. The first ascent is up Mount Success and on to the White Mountains.

  The remainder of the New Hampshire trail is in the Crescent Range near the town of Randolph, New

Hampshire. The "Founding Father" peaks all stand within the Presidential Range of the White Mountains. "Rugged and inspiring,"[56] New Hampshire possesses more miles of trail over the tree line than in any other state. The state holds 106 miles of the total distance and features the worst weather in the trail's entirety, especially when storms hit. The mountains are steep and test the hiker's knee strength. The alpine tundra is "fragile,"[57] and open areas present a special danger to hikers in the form of rock falls.

The Dartmouth Outing Club is another strong force for maintenance of the Appalachian Trail in New Hampshire. Established in 1909, it is the largest and oldest collegiate outing club in America. In the years between 1910 and 1930, it grew to such size as to require subdividing by outdoor interest, affiliating with other outdoor groups by activity.

Dartmouth only notes, "Anyone – member or not – may stay at our cabins, go on our trips, rent our gear, and take our classes."[58] Originally initiated to "stimulate interest in out-of-door winter sports,"[59] the program grew to a membership of 1,500 student members. The club establishes trips, provides outdoor leadership and

---

[56] Appalachian Trail Conservancy, Welcome to New Hampshire – www.appalachiantrail.org/explore/explore-by-state/new-hampshire/
[57] Appalachian Trail Conservancy
[58] Dartmouth Outdoors, About the Dartmouth Outing Club – www.outdoors.dartmouth/doc/
[59] Dartmouth Outdoors

distributes medical and safety information while maintaining a 50-mile stretch of the Appalachian National Scenic Trail. It has become an umbrella organization for a dozen member clubs each specializing in an aspect of outdoor recreation.

More than half a century following its establishment, the college created the Department of Outdoor Affairs to relieve the club of its administrative burdens. It was later renamed the Outdoor Programs Office. The Appalachian Trail runs through Hanover, New Hampshire, home of Dartmouth College, before entering the state of Vermont across the Connecticut River.

The trail winds through 150 miles of Vermont, entering from the south-central border with New Hampshire and traveling to the mid-state before turning southwest to the southwestern border with Massachusetts. It boasts a significant rise in elevation, from 400 to 4,000 feet.

The primary caretaker for the Vermont Appalachian Trail is the same organization that tends the Long Trail that coincides with the Appalachian for much of the distance within the state. They remain contiguous within the Green Mountains for a distance of 95 miles. The Green Mountain Club is the primary caretaker of both trails. The Long Trail is the oldest long-distance hiking trail within the United States. It was conceived by James

P. Taylor (1872-1949), who first imagined it while waiting for the mist to dissipate on the summit of Stratton Mountain.

   The first signs of action concerning the Vermont trail occurred at the end of the first decade of the century at a March 11 meeting in Burlington. In the following decade, work began in Camel's Hump and the Mount Mansfield areas. Only two years later, a path was cleared from Camel's Hump to Sterling Pond. Within the following decade, members of the Green Mountain Club had built 209 miles of trail and had provided 44 overnight facilities. In the 1930s, a final link was cut to the Canadian line. The club celebrated the trail's 21st birthday with a large party and lit flares from mountain top to mountain top of the Green Mountain peaks.

   Once the trail was completed, work turned to an increase in shelters, an effort led by Roy O. Buchanan and groups of students. The Green Mountain Club's protection of the trail through Vermont has been heroic at times. In the mid-1930s, a parallel scenic highway was proposed, to which the club mounted an "energetic opposition,"[60] causing the plan to be rejected in a statewide forum. An effort by the Air Force to build a missile signaling station atop Mount Mansfield 20 years later was similarly beaten back by the Green Mountain Club. The organization has

[60] The Green Mountain Club, Long Trail, 1910 – www.greenmountainclub.org/about/thegreenmountainclub/

largely remained silent on national conservation issues, dedicating itself to preserving the character of the Long Trail. In the years after World War II, shelter construction had reached 61 facilities. Responding to heavy hiker traffic on the trail, the club responded by removing dumps from facilities, initiating a carry in-carry out policy, and a host of other initiatives. A decade later, the Vermont State Legislature officially recognized the Green Mountain Club as the "founder, sponsor, defender and protector"[61] of the entire Long Trail System.

Among the most popular sites along the Vermont Trail is Mt. Killington, the location of the "bunk house" for through-hikers, with a "breath-taking viewpoint."[62]

The Appalachian Trail moves through Massachusetts in its western region, from an entry point near Williamstown. It proceeds in a north-to-south direction from the Vermont to Connecticut borders in the Berkshire Range. It then crosses the Hoosic and the Housatonic Rivers.

Although there are several other organizations that contribute to the trail's care in Massachusetts, such as a southeastern chapter of the Appalachian Trail Club, most duties are under the wing of the AMC-Western

---

[61] The Green Mountain Club

[62] Blue Ridge Outdoors, 10 Stunning Viewpoints Along the Appalachian Trail – www.blueridgeoutdoors.com/go-outside/10-stunning-viewpoints-along-appalachian-trail/

Massachusetts. Its mission is to maintain the entire 90-mile stretch of the trail that moves through four counties. These include Berkshire, Franklin, Hampshire, and Hampden. Formerly the Berkshire Club, they reorganized and grew into activity committees drawn from the general membership. The Western Massachusetts Mountain Club is part of the Appalachian Conservancy.

The 90-mile stretch through Massachusetts features "expansive highlands, distinctive mountains, layered ridgelines, lush river walks and shaded glens."[63] This is all a part of experiencing the Berkshire Range, which rises from 650 feet to 3,491 feet in elevation. Massachusetts is home to Mount Everett in the south and Greylock to the north. Greylock is known as the mountain that inspired Herman Melville to write *Moby Dick*. On a clear day, visitors can see clear views up to 90 miles. From the summit of Baldpate, people can view two "incredible summits"[64] overlooking the "rolling mountains"[65] of Massachusetts.

The membership is comprised of approximately 2,900 self-reliant hikers. Those traveling from the south will experience a significant change of terrain after the hills of the mid-Atlantic states. The change can first be felt on the

---

[63] Appalachian Trail Conservancy, Welcome to Massachusetts – www.appalachiantrail.org/explore/explore-by-state/massachusetts/
[64] Blue Ridge Outdoors
[65] Blue Ridge Outdoors

rocky slopes of Bear Mountain at the Connecticut border. Through 91 miles, the hiker will "traverse rugged peaks and soothing seas of conifers, explore charming New England towns and dip in swimming holes."[66] A great deal of elevation change occurs throughout the Massachusetts portion.

A particular highlight of the Massachusetts trail is the Sages Ravine, a series of cascades and deep pools. Others include Mount Race, Mt. Everett, and location of the Last Battle of Shay's Rebellion, in which disgruntled Massachusetts citizens mounted an uprising against the fledgling U.S. governments taxation policies. That incident led to the formation of our modern Constitution. The trail town of Great Barrington features an interesting and energized downtown area. The peak of Bear Mountain as the trail passes through the Taconic Range following the Housatonic takes it through several state parks.

The trail passes from Massachusetts to Connecticut from the brook crossing at Sages Ravine to Sherman at the New York state line at a distance of 48.6 miles. The elevation varies from 260 to 2,316 feet. A three-quarter mile stretch along the Housatonic River was the first section to become universally accessible. It is located on a flat section located in Falls Village, the site of a former iron

---

[66] The Trek

forge below a 50-foot waterfall. The Connecticut chapter boasts 8,000 members. The trail passes through the northwest corner of the state.

Most of the Connecticut route was blazed by Ned K. Anderson, the Connecticut Forest and Park Association's Chairman of the Housatonic Valley section, in the late 1920s. The route travels down the Housatonic Valley and crosses the river twice. This portion of the trail features "forested landscapes, rugged rocky hills, open valleys, ravines, waterfalls, and magnificent vistas."[67] Wildflowers abound in spring and summer, and hikers can see turkey, deer, and fox year-round.

The New York State portion of the Appalachian Trail crosses into the state from New Jersey and runs through the southern portion for approximately 92 miles at an elevation between 124 and 1,433 feet. The most unique feature of the New York segment of the trail is that it passes New York City 30 miles to the south once it has crossed the Hudson, barely above sea level. This offers hikers a simultaneous view of verdant woods and the Manhattan skyline. Passing through Harriman-Bear State Park, it heads south through the newly protected Sterling Forest. An unexpected display of wildlife can be found on the New York trail as it passes through the Trailside Museum and a zoo at Bear Mountain. At 124 feet in

[67] Connecticut Forest & Park Association, Appalachian Trail – www.ctwoodlands.org/blue-blazed-hiking-trails/appalachian-trail

elevation, Bear Mountain is the lowest point of the entire distance.

The volunteer-powered New York – New Jersey Trail Conference builds, maintains, and protects the trail with 200 plus volunteers. The mission statement of the Conference holds that all people "regardless of age, ability, or location"[68] should be able to experience the rewards that connect them to nature. The New York trail is "not a leisurely walk in the park"[69] as some believe, but a hike requiring thorough research.

In New Jersey, the route runs along the northern border for 72 miles. It passes through the Wallkill National Wildlife Reserve and the Wayawanda Park to Hike Point State Park. It then follows the Kitatinny Ridge past Sunfish Pond on its way to the Delaware Water Gap. Sightings of the state bird, the eastern goldfinch, are common along the New Jersey segment. The elevation is classified as easy to moderate, moving from 350 to 1,685 feet. Hikers will be required to cross bogs and wetlands. Reaching one's destination is important, as camping is restricted to designated sites, and campfires outside of designated facilities are prohibited.

The trail enters Pennsylvania from New Jersey at the central east border at the Delaware Water Gap and follows

[68] New York-New Jersey Trail Conference, Welcome to the New York-New Jersey Trail Conference – www.nynjtc.org

the eastern rim of the Alleghenies. The elevation statewide is 320 to 2,080 feet, and the trail becomes increasingly rocky. Pennsylvania is affectionately nicknamed "Rocksylvania," although the trail is not entirely rocky. The southern section offers some of the gentlest and smoothest terrain of the entire trail, especially in Cumberland Valley.

At the mid-point is the Pennsylvania Appalachian Trail Museum in Pine Grove State Park. The charming town of Boiling Springs houses the Appalachian Trail Conservancy's mid-Atlantic office. Much of the trail passes through game lands managed for hunting, so autumn is not the optimum time for hiking the trail. Hunters and non-hunters alike are required to wear 250 square inches of fluorescent orange on the head, chest, and back, or an orange hat. Only through-hikers, those who set out at a beginning point, to any exit point may camp on Pennsylvania Game Commission lands between 200 feet from the trail and 500 feet from a stream or spring.

The Potomac Appalachian Trail Club covers 240 miles of Appalachian Trail in Virginia, West Virginia, Maryland and Pennsylvania. The Keystone Trails Association represents the interests and concerns of the Pennsylvania hiking community. Pennsylvania is known for its many support groups. The Cumberland Valley Appalachian

Trail Club maintains 17 miles through the valley between Carlisle and Mechanicsburg to the top of Blue Mountain. The York Hiking Club maintains a 13-mile section on Blue Mountain and a 7.5-mile section a few miles north of Harrisburg.

The Susquehanna Gap Trail Club volunteers contribute over 2,000 hours per year on a 20-mile section running from PA-225 on Peters Mountain north to Rausch Gap. This famous club organizes over one hundred hikes per year for every skill level.

The Allentown Hiking Club is sponsored by the Allentown Recreation Bureau and is a member organization of the Keystone Trail Association and Appalachian Trail Conference. The Allentown club maintains 10.3 miles of Appalachian Trail and two backcountry shelters north of New Tripoli and G.W. Outerbridge west of Lehigh Gap.

The Blue Mountain Eagle Climbing Club cleans and repairs several sections of the Appalachian Trail, its shelters, and the Arboretum. Even the state of Delaware has a cooperative association with the Pennsylvania entities, despite the fact that the trail does not pass through that state. Known as the Wilmington Trail Club, and membership includes 600 members from Delaware, Pennsylvania, Maryland, and New Jersey. It schedules over 400 events per year, lasting from a few hours to a few days. The AMC Delaware Valley Chapter was founded in 1876, and the Batona Hiking Club of Philadelphia serves the city and its surrounding communities.

Of the major sites in Pennsylvania, the Pinnacle situated on the Blue Mountain Ridgeline is of particular interest. The trail completes its course through Pennsylvania into Cumberland Valley and diagonals through the southeastern corner of the state before crossing into Maryland in the central south.

Leaving Pennsylvania, the trail runs to the south-central border of Maryland and West Virginia. The Maryland portion of the trail, spanning 40.6 miles, follows the crests of the South Mountain. At one point, it comes down to briefly join the historic C&O Canal for a few miles before crossing the Potomac.

By trail standards, the Maryland segment is easy traveling, being at an average of 1,650 feet in elevation. In general, the mid-Atlantic states are gentler in terrain and elevation changes. The region is approximately 430 miles across and can be accomplished in around 32 days.

The low point is on the Potomac River at 250 feet, rising to 1,900 feet at High Rock. Maryland offers fewer steep climbs, but some "impressive scenery."[70] Hikers in

Maryland can begin or end treks from literally hundreds of points between the northern and southern ends. Crossing the state can be accomplished in three to five days, and shelters are spaced a day apart.

Popular day hikes abound, and one can begin or end a hike from literally hundreds of locations between the northern and southern ends. Among the favorites are one from Greenbrier State Park to Annapolis Rock, and Black Rock to the Washington Monument State Park. Another popular route is from Gathland State Park to Weaverton Cliffs. The elevation at Annapolis Rock is 1,700 feet, while the Washington Monument State Park is 1,600. Weaverton Cliffs stands at only 750 feet.

Several historic sites are to be found in the Maryland segment, including the original Washington Monument and the War Correspondents Monument. The southernmost three miles follow the historic Chesapeake & Ohio Canal Towpath on the Potomac. The best time to hike Maryland is mid-April through mid-May. The Potomac Appalachian Club is the "premiere hiking group in the state."[71]

Winding into Virginia once it has crossed the Potomac, the Appalachian Trail enters the largest segment of its

---

[70] Appalachian Trail, Maryland Park Service, Department of Natural Resources –
    www.dnr.maryland.gov/publiclands/Pages/at.aspx

[71] Appalachian Trail Conservancy, Welcome to Maryland – www.apptrail.org/explore/expore-by-state/maryland/

length, containing the most miles of any state on the trail, 531, sharing 25 of them with the West Virginia border. Virginia's distance equals approximately one quarter of the entire distance, and the elevation rises from 265 to 5,500 feet. This makes for relatively easy elevation changes and good "tread." Many hikers in good condition "crank out"[72] up to 20 miles per day. Along the way, after crossing the Shenandoah River, the trail ties in with the magnificent Shenandoah National Park, the Skyline drive, and parallels the Blue Ridge Parkway.

The Shenandoah segment contains 104 miles of well-maintained trails. It continues southward through the Mount Rogers National Recreation Area in the George Washington and Jefferson National Forests. In the Jefferson National Forest, hikers encounter McAfee Knob, and an ascent to 1,740 feet above the Shenandoah Valley. Dragon's Tooth, an aptly named rock monolith of Tuscarora quartz sits above Cove Mountain at 1,505 feet, which straddles Craig and Roanoke counties just west of Catawba. Mount Moosilauke summits at 4,802 feet, offering a panoramic view of the surrounding mountains. In the southeastern corner of the state is Grayson Highlands State Park, considered the best bouldering site in Virginia. Grayson Park is located near Mount Rogers and Whitetop Mountain, Virginia's two highest peaks,

____

[72] Michael Lanza, Backpacker Outside

sitting at over 5,000 feet in elevation. Wild ponies run free there and are readily visible from the trail.

The Virginia trail ends in Damascus, known as "Trail Town, USA," passing down the main throughfare. In the northern portion of Virginia, key sites include a stint along the Virginia/West Virginia border, an ideal hiking area for students, perfect for spring break. In the first 54 miles, a hiker will travel through Sky Meadows State Park, the Richard Thompson Wildlife Management area, and the Bears Den Trail Center.

In the central portion of the state, the trail accompanies the Blue Ridge Parkway all the way to Roanoke, becoming increasingly difficult as one travels southward. It completes a 225-mile stretch of trail in the central region through the Washington and Jefferson Forests, by the Peaks of Otter, and the Blue Ridge Parkway.

In the southernmost region, the trail takes a westerly direction, remaining in the Washington and Jefferson forests, the most remote and little-traveled portion of Virginia. The southern trail extends 166 miles. The best time for hiking this section is May to October, with premier sites such as Big Walker Lookout, the Mount Rogers Scenic Byway, and the Grayson Highlands State Park. Driving by car along the parallel route, one crosses the Appalachian Trail 30 times.

Backcountry permits are required when passing through the various state parks to fund maintenance. Like Pennsylvania, Virginia features a myriad of support groups. They include the Potomac Appalachian Trail Club, the Old Dominion Appalachian Trail Club, the Tidewater Appalachian Trail Club, the Natural Bridge Appalachian Trail Club, the Outdoor Club at Virginia Tech., the Roanoke Appalachian Trail Club, the Piedmont Appalachian Trail Hikers, the Mount Rogers Appalachian Trail Club, and the ATC Volunteer Program.

The Potomac Appalachian Trail Club has been active since 1927 and covers much of the mid-Atlantic region. The Old Dominion Club focuses mostly on Virginia hiking, but also promotes biking, paddling and rowing. The Tidewater Club is open to individuals and their families and manages a ten mile stretch of the Appalachian Trail. Centered in Norfolk, membership comes mostly from Hampton Roads and the surrounding area. The Natural Bridge Appalachian Trail Club is a volunteer-based hiking club that maintains over 90 miles of the Appalachian Trail, and other prominent trails of central Virginia. The Outdoor Club of Virginia Tech is made up of numerous undergraduates and graduates, along with other members of the Blacksburg community. Their focus is to get their members to be active, both "physically and socially."[73]

The Appalachian Trail north of Pearisburg, including Rice Field/Peters Mountain, is maintained by the Old Dominion Club. The Roanoke Appalachian Trail Club was founded in 1932 for "avid hikers and backpackers."[74] It maintains 120 miles of Appalachian Trail and 16 of its shelters. Offering two group hikes each week with invited guests, it focuses on the Appalachian Trail to the south of Pearisburg, including Angels Rest/Pearis Mountain. The Piedmont Appalachian Trail Hikers maintains a section of the trail in southwestern Virginia. Members live in North Carolina and Virginia, with the majority between Charlottesville and Raleigh. Volunteers of the the Mount Rogers Appalachian Trail Club cover 59.4 miles from the Tennessee/Virginia line to South Fork of the Holston Bridge, Rte. 670 to Teas, Virginia. The ATC Volunteer Programs recruit workers to perform general maintenance on various trails of the state.

The West Virginia segment of the trail stretches only 2.4 miles within the state, and another 25 along the West Virginia/Virginia border. The trail dips across the line in southwestern Virginia, at a point where the elevation lies between 265 and 1,200 feet. It passes through the heart of the Harpers Ferry National Historic Park, site of John Brown's famous raid.

[73] Appalachian Trail Conservancy, Welcome to Virginia – www.appalachiantrail.org/explore/explore-by-state/virginia/

[74] Appalachian Trail Conservancy, Welcome to Virginia

The West Virginia segment passing through Harpers Ferry houses the headquarters of the Appalachian Trail Conservancy at the national level, with a Visitors Center where hikers have their photos taken and log their travels. It is known to travelers as the "psychological halfway point"[75] of the national trail, not so much in terms of distance, but as a transition between north and south.

In Harpers Ferry, the trail passes through the former Storer College, created as a base of education for freed enslaved people after the Civil War. No camping is permitted in Harpers Ferry, or in the National Historic Park, but numerous B&Bs and nearby campgrounds are available. West Virginia features the shortest distance of any state but is among the most well-known.

---

[75] Appalachian Trail Conservancy, Welcome to West Virginia – www.appalachiantrail.org/explore.explore-by-state/west-virginia/

A picture of part of the trail around Harpers Ferry

The magnificent Tennessee countryside of the eastern portion of the state inspired the direction of the route with its "sun-dappled forests, unobstructed "balds" and high elevation summits carpeted in natural grasses."[76] The state contains a 94-mile stretch within its borders, and another 260 miles along the Tennessee/North Carolina line. The elevation range is among the greatest of all the states, ranging from 1,326 to 6,625 feet. As the 94 miles ascends toward the High Country near the state line, hikers traverse the highest mountains of the trail, with several over 6,000 feet. The primary attraction of the Tennessee trail is the Great Smoky Mountains National Park, which

[76] Appalachian Trail Conservancy, Welcome to Tennessee – www.appalachiantrail.org/explore/explore-by-state/tennessee/

requires advance permits, and other shelter permits depending on the proposed length of the hike.

The Smoky Mountain Hiking Club was founded in the mid-1920s and is among the oldest and largest organizations of its kind in the southeastern United States. The model was inspired by several of Tennessee's native sons, including Harvey Broome, Carlos Campbell, Jim Thompson, Dutch Roth, and others. The Smoky Mountain Hiking Club tends 102 miles of the Appalachian Trail, both in the Smokies and the Nantahala National Forest.

The club was established with the assistance of the Knoxville YMCA, through the sponsorship of an adult hiking program. Subsequent meetings led to the present-day organization. The first scheduled hike reached the summit of Mount LeConte on December 6, 1924 with a group of eight. Traversing the Great Smoky Mountains takes approximately seven days. During that trek, hikers will reach Clingman's Dome in North Carolina, the highest point of elevation on the entire trail. From Clingman's Dome, the terrain drops into the "dark and steep walls of the Nantahala River Gorge."[77]

North Carolina hosts 96.4 miles of trail within the state, and another 217 miles on the Tennessee/North Carolina border. The Carolina Mountain Club, the oldest hiking

[77] Appalachian Trail Conservancy, Welcome to North Carolina – www.appalachiantrail.org/explore/explore-by-state/north-carolina/

and trail monitoring club in western North Carolina, maintains 92.6 miles of the Appalachian Trail from Davenport Gap to Spivey Gap. The Hot Springs Mountain Club tends to the various trails connected to Hot Springs, while the Nantahala Hiking Club serves as one of the 31 volunteer Appalachian Trail groups in the national Conservancy. The NHC tends to 58.6 miles of the trail from Bly Gap at the North Carolina/Georgia border to the Nantahala Outdoor Center on the Nantahala River at Wesser, North Carolina. It also tends to various trails connected with the Appalachian Trail.

Leaving Tennessee, one reaches the summit of fire-tower capped peaks near Franklin before crossing Fontana Dam at the exit from the Smokies. Travelers then climb Roan Mountain and into the Roan Highlands.

Among the favorite stopping points in North Carolina is Max Patch, a grassy mountain top with an abundance of wildflowers and berries during the appropriate seasons. The short loop on Max Patch enables a 360-degree panorama. Another favorite hike takes the backpacker from Lemon Gap to Max Patch by an alternate route, through a wildflower-filled creek valley. Along the way, one can visit Roaring Fork Shelter and hike the trail from Deep Gap near Franklin to the beautiful views at Standing Indian Mountain Summit. This route takes one through "rhododendron tunnels"[78] and views of the Tallulah

River's headwaters to Lake Burton.

Hot Springs to Lover's Leap is only two miles in length, but quite steep. Travelers arrive at Lovers Leap Waterfall and a rocky precipice that legend holds was the site of a fateful fall of a "heartbroken Cherokee Princess."[79] More than in most other segments of the trail, the hiker will feel a deep sense of remoteness. Bly Gap to Fontana Dam is an 88-mile hike up the entrance of the Smokies. Another 88 miles in the Smokies section covers the Appalachian Trail inside the National Park from Fontana Dam to the park entrance. Davenport Gap to US-19E runs 151 miles along the Tennessee/North Carolina border.

North Carolina and Tennessee are generally referenced as one state in the bulk of materials on the trail. However, the North Carolina section sports the densest gathering of black bears in the eastern United States. The trees of old growth timber in North Carolina have been described as "massive and prehistoric."[80] The mountains out of Tennessee rise to "spectacular summits"[81] such as Clingman's Dome at 6,343 feet, the tallest peak on the trail, offering a scant 10 miles per day advancement to most hikers.

Once in the Smokies, 15 miles per day is possible.

---

[78] Asheville Trails, Appalachian trail in North Carolina – www.ashevilletrails.com/appalachian-trail-north-carolina/
[79] Asheville Trails
[80] Asheville Trails
[81] Asheville Trails

Clingman's Dome offers hikers a 360-degree view above the tree line of the Smokey Mountains, and on a clear day, one can view seven states. The trail comes down into Georgia from the upper northeast to the upper central portion of the state through the Nantahala Forest.

The northern mountains are nothing like the rest of Georgia. The highest peak is 4,161 feet, three times the height of the Empire State Building, and the lowest elevation is 2,500 feet in height, higher than any point on the trail between Northern Virginia and Massachusetts. No peanut farms or peach trees exist in this part of the state, but the land is occupied with five federally designated wilderness areas.

In March and early April, the Appalachian Trail in Georgia can be frigid and crowded. The mountains can be "miserably cold."[82] The snowfall and cold can rival lower mountains a thousand miles north on the trail, and cold snaps can fall into single digits.

The Georgia Appalachian Trail Club protects all trails with volunteers, with an emphasis on conservation. The ATC Program works on the Appalachian Trail, assisting in the Visitors Center and headquarters. Formed in 1930, all of the Appalachian Trail in Georgia is contained within the Chattahoochee and Oconee National Forest.

---

[82] Appalachian Trail in Georgia, US Department of Agriculture, National Forest Service –
www.fs.usda.gov/recrea/conf/recarea?recrea=62815

As the year's new crop of hikers prepares to leave Georgia for points north, they soon meet their north-to-south colleagues at or near Springer Mountain or at Amicola Springs, an added eight-mile approach hike. The trail is marked by two-inch to six-inch vertical painted blazes.

The Georgia trail proceeds northward to the Blue Ridge Wildlife Management Area, as it passes through five federally designated wilderness areas. The southern terminus begins on the expansive rock outcrop Springer Mountain of 3,782 feet. A plaque that reads "Georgia to Maine – a footpath for those who seek fellowship with the wilderness"[83] is embedded in the mountain. A stretch of 76.4 miles is protected by a one-mile boundary by agreement of the U.S. Forest Service and the U.S. Park Service.

The GTC Ambassador Program lends assistance to hikers on the trail. The Georgia thru-hiker jacket patch is available to any who have walked the entire distance through Georgia. It is not necessary to be a member. Progress in the mountainous areas of Georgia is calculated optimistically in much of the reference material, but to make eight miles per day is fair progress. Along the way, five highways intersect the trail, but otherwise the hiking feels remote. The highest points in the state include Blood

[83] Appalachian Trail in Georgia

Mountain at 4,485 feet, and Tray Mountain at 4,430.

Through central and northern Georgia, the trail follows the eastern ridge of the Appalachians. Before reaching the ridge, the first town that hikers come across from the southern terminus is Dahlonga. The town is famous for its "Trail Days" celebrations, bringing musicians, authors and speakers from all over to gather with outdoor enthusiasts. The Appalachian Trail Club manages and maintains the trail in cooperation with the Conservancy and the U.S. Forest Service, providing a wide range of activities for its members.

The youngest person ever to cross Georgia, then complete the entire trail all the way to Maine was Harry Sutton, who accomplished this feat in 209 days at the age of five.

Materials and symbols to mark the trail have included embossed copper squares with the trail insignia. However, these became easy prey for souvenir hunters, so Perkins designed a diamond-shaped galvanized iron marker with the trail monogram, which was rubber-stamped and then varnished. The main reliance on marking the trail is a rectangular paint blaze of a few inches square placed fore and aft in the direction of travel – blue for side trails and yellow in New Jersey and New York. Blue is the color for Connecticut and one small section of Vermont. There is only one approved symbol, a double blaze, two superimposed blazes or markers, with a warning of obscure turns or changes of direction.

The Appalachian Trail in Popular Culture

An array of literature has continued to be published about or inspired by the trail, with its endless source of nature, wilderness, and its "romantic past."[84] Travel Writer Horace Kephart was active in the Smoky Mountain Club during the first days and wrote a memoir of his time in the Smoky Mountains. In the early century, he published a guide to camping and woodcraft. Originally a Pennsylvanian raised in Iowa, he worked for Yale University as a librarian. During that time, he penned a study of Appalachian culture. Eventually, he was called upon to help chart the course of the Appalachian Trail through the Great Smoky National Park.

Equally on the informative side of the Appalachian Trail literature are five guidebooks that have kept pace with new construction through the years. The fifth has yet to be published, as the publishers await the completion of a new trail in the Smokies. The Appalachian Trail Conference has issued a new comprehensive pamphlet, including information on a series of shelters spread ten miles apart, largely in the north for day hikers. In the present day,

hikers are fully informed on the most remote segments of
the trail, able to walk the lonely 173 miles in Maine in 17
days, finding a new shelter each night.

Bill Bryson's *A Walk in the Woods* caused a serious
backlash among offended southerners who became fed up
with the myth that "everyone in the South is a hick."[85]
While it is true that the book was advertised as a
"hilarious travelogue"[86] and lampoons all the characters
and their cultures, it became well-known in the nonfiction
section by naming "loony hillbillies"[87] as a selling point.
In the end, it was considered to be "fairly useless"[88] as a
travel guide, described in one review as a "useless
purchase."[89] Later, it was turned into a feature film of the
same title, with Robert Redford playing Bryson and Nick
Nollte as his hiking companion. Much of the film was
shot in Georgia including scenes at Amicola Falls State
Park and Neels Gap, and as well as in Buford and
Kennesaw. *Walking on the Clouds* (1939) of Almer C.
Adams was the first account of a hiker who completed the
entire trail.

With passage of the National Trails Act in 1968, the trail
was transformed from "regional grassroots endeavor"[90] to

---

[85] Mary Jean Ronan Herzog, Including Appalachian Stereotypes in Multicultural Education: An Analysis of Bill Bryson's A Walk in the Woods, *Journal of Appalachian Studies* Vol. 5 No. 1 (Spring 1998)

[86] Mary Jean Ronan Herzog

[87] Mary Jean Ronan Herzog

[88] Mary Jean Ronan Herzog

[89] Mary Jean Ronan Herzog

[90] Sarah Middlefehldt, The People's Path: Conflict and Cooperation in the Acquisition of the Appalachian Trail: *Environmental*

an important part of the National Park System. The political bent for and against the trail was an odd assortment of interests. It received support from "Baptist ministers and MIT professors, postal clerks and American presidents."[91] Resistance was strong, however, from chicken farmers and property rights advocates, land developers, and libertarians."[92] The "people's path" became the new moniker as public and private boundaries became blurred, creating a new institutional model for land conversation known as the "public-private partnership."[93]

McKaye had envisioned two kinds of paths. One was to exist outside the range of motor sounds to be made by "amateur workers…a "squirrel track type."[94] The other was to be placed within a thin zone of motor sounds created by a government labor force, "a graded type."[95] At the time, private land depended on handshakes between volunteers and the Appalachian Trail Conference landowners. The result of postwar pressures, many miles of original trail obliterated or relocated on new roads guaranteed that the informal agreements would no longer suffice. The 1968 National Trails ACT fixed all of that.

History, Vol. 15, No. 4 (October 2010)

[91] Sarah Middlefehldt

[92] Sarah Middlefehldt

[93] Sarah Middlefehldt

[94] Sarah Middlefehldt

[95] Sarah Middlefehldt

In 1974, the Appalachian Trail Conservancy commissioned a greenway study in preparation for the trail's 50th anniversary celebrations. Ann Satterthwaite authored a report on the state of the trail that recommended a return to MacKaye's original vision. Satterthwaite's report received outward approval, and even open endorsement, but at the completion of the path itself, the concept faded in the minds of those in power. Today, however, a 280,000 acre "green ribbon"[96] exists, connecting federal and state conservation lands of the eastern United States. Nearly 100% of it is protected by a passageway at least 500 feet to either side of the trail. With the advance of new technologies, overseeing organizations fight to keep the trail from experiencing the "smells and sounds of urban life"[97] such as those of utility lines and wind towers. Some of MacKaye's original principles remain in this conflict. He stated at a 1933 conference the entire experience should be a "realm and not merely a trail."[98]

In 1978, the document was dramatically altered in terms of increased appropriations, which grew from five million to 90 million. The width of safety corridor was increased from 200 feet to 1000 feet. These were hard-fought battles. Land acquisition in the eastern portion of the U.S.

---

[96] Dennis Schaffer, Connecting Humans and Nature: The Appalachian Trail Landscape Conservation Initiate, *The George Wright Forum* Vol. 133 No. 2 (2016)

[97] Dennis Schaffer

[98] Sarah Middlefehldt

was a good deal more difficult than in the west. Landowners fought against it with commercialism on the rise, but the Park Service instituted a series of "get tough" policies. These made it far easier to eliminate, condemn, or diminish businesses that marred the landscape.

The actual act of hiking any segment of the trail has been promoted in much finer detail in the intervening years. As a reminder that hiking much of the trail is a remote experience, the dangers are enumerated in the new literature, with extensive printed solutions available.

As of 2021, a great deal of trailhead parking has been added, and overnight shelters have been upgraded, thanks in large part to Appalachian Trail communities and trail clubs. As of that year, long distance hiking has once more been deemed safe in terms of the Covid epidemic, especially for the vaccinated. However, the Norovirus has received conversation of late, and people are urged to protect against infected individuals, contaminated food or water, or touching contaminated surfaces. The incidence of the disease is thus far at a low number.

Being in the beauty of nature does not make hikers immune to crime, both petty and violent, although the latter is rare. In sites with much human traffic, the Appalachian Trail Conservancy has positioned more "ridge runners"[99] for public education. They serve as "caretakers,"[100] with two-way radios, acting as "eyes and ears."[101] Still, hikers must be aware that in many remote areas, help is far away, and that the Appalachian Trail Conservancy has no mechanism with which to effect law enforcement.

Travelers are urged to let important people know their plans in advance. On long distance hikes, a copy of a hiker's itinerary should be left behind, with a description of one's gear for your contact person. Many believe that to take along a dog is a guarantee of safety, but this can lead to a false sense of security, especially if an attacker is armed. It is legal to possess firearms on the trail. The owner must also be certain of controlling his dog's urges to pursue animals.

The use of trail shelter registers so that one's whereabouts can be determined is important. Regular online journals are recommended. The Forest Service urges its travelers to avoid hitchhiking or accepting rides when the trail meets paved roads.

There are natural dangers on the trail as well. The use of bear cannisters is recommended, a manner of packing food difficult for the animals to smell. Some states allow bear bags separate and high up from campsites. A few of

---

[99] NPS, National Park Service Appalachian Scenic Trail – www.nps.gov/apps/planyourvisit/safety.htm

[100] NPS National Park Service

[101] NPS National Park Service

the snakes found in the Appalachians are venomous and are not to be agitated. Timber rattlers and copperheads are among the most prevalent poisonous snakes along the trail.

While the literature assures potential hikers that bears "rarely confront people,"[102] such instances do occur. They will usually smell a human long before he arrives, and deliberate noise is recommended, such as talking, singing, or ringing a bell. Other animals commonly encountered include foxes, boars, racoons, porcupines, coyotes, wood ducks, bobcats, chipmunks, river otters, beavers, squirrels, woodchucks, warblers, hawks, and owls. Foxes, bats, and racoons are the most likely to carry rabies. Of the ticks, mosquitos, and black flies, ticks are the most problematic. They are in 14 states and thrive between 2,000 and 3,000 feet. They are common in Vermont and Virginia between the months of May and July.

Travelers are reminded that the trail was designed to bring people to the mountains, so when there is a choice between the trail going around or over one, up is usually the choice. Some portions pass through state parks that charge fees locally, with some permits free for through-hikers.

Every hiker has a different physique and load-carrying

---

[102] Trailheads, Hiking the Appalachian Trail, The Complete Guide for Beginners in 2021- www.trailheads.com/blog/appalachian-trail-complete-guide

capacity, but the Forest Service recommends a pack weight around 20 to 25 pounds. It must be carefully packed and should use the most modern materials possible so as not to add unnecessary weight. Gear should include a tent and sleeping bag; and a trowel, first aid kit, bear cannister, and repair kit; cooking utensils, a compass, maps, and a flashlight; as well as undergarments, and clothing accessories for changes in temperature, humidity, and weather. The basic list continues with rain gear, socks, shoes, and a light jacket; Also, Vaseline, bug repellant, duct tape, trash bags, biodegradable soap and toothpaste; and finally, a whistle, waterproof matches, water filter, and extra batteries.

Literature enumerates the dangers of setting out on a spartan hike following a period of inactivity. Yoga is an excellent preparation for flexibility, and trail running for cardio and lung function. Climbing for strength, swimming for joints, and stair climbing is recommended for cardio, lung and elevation changes. The recommended diet is high-calorie, approximately 2,500 to 4,500 calories per day. Eating is recommended as much and as often as possible. Dry food should be repackaged into small lightweight units, and well-sealed containers, in lieu of heavier liquids. Some of the food should be eaten before setting out, and an occasional reward treat should be packed. Finding water is not usually difficult, but some states feature longer water carries, periods in which water must be transported for longer distances, especially during dry spells. Flowing water should always be chosen over stagnant water, and it must be treated and purified.

It is estimated that the average cost for walking the trail efficiently is around $1,000 per month. It may cost one to two thousand for original gear, but second-hand is satisfactory. In many areas, hiker boxes are available along the route, and hikers are urged to leave whatever is unnecessary for others. On occasions where one spends a night in town, spending $50 to $100 per day is on the average to be expected. A figure of $1,500 should be set aside for contingency money.

All in all, the modern trail covers eight national forests and six national park units, two national wildlife refuges, and 24 wilderness areas. The trail contains eight national landmarks, three national historic landmarks, and 60 state protected areas, 88 counties, 168 townships and municipalities. The trail "transcends traditional boundaries and jurisdictional designations.[103] The next goal is to transform the country's perception into that of an ongoing system, rather than a long, thin corridor divided by artificial lines, thereby "broadening the scale of protection."[104]

---

[103] Dennis Shaffer
[104] Dennis Shaffer

When the rare hiker finishes the distance from Georgia to Maine or in reverse, he or she has made an elevation change of several hundred thousand feet, approximately the equal of scaling Mt. Everest 17 times. Since the trail's inception, 20,000 hikers have completed the distance, including 700 over the age of 60, and 50 over the age of 70. From either direction, the "green tunnel" known as the Appalachian Trail is both accessible and beautiful in every state. In the north, it is fashioned from forest mix of deciduous and coniferous, of fir, spruce, and maple, buckeye, beech, birch, oak, and white oak. In the south, it is poplar, hickory, walnut, and sycamore. On the western slopes of the Smokies, it is chestnut, hemlock, and oaks. In the upper south, it is berries, wildflowers, fungi, ferns, and tulips.

Volunteers continue to be the trail's most abiding and striking feature. The story of the trail contrasts other such projects, "a story filled with good fortune, good will, and almost miraculous accomplishments."[105] Where original agreements were based on handshakes with landowners, ten years into the project saw Appalachian Trail Agreements appear. These were signed by the National Park Service with the Forest Service and the ATC as partners to protect lands adjacent to the footpath. Subsequent agreements saw the buffer go to one half mile.

---

[105] Pamela Underhill, The Appalachian Scenic Trail: A Neverending Story, *The George Wright Forum*, Vol. 6 No. 2 (1989) George Wright Society

In the past 40 years since the 1970s, there has been an acquisition of 78,000 acres of new land in more than 50 counties in eleven states, resulting in permanent protection of over 500 miles.

Several issues exist with recalcitrant ski resort operators in New England, whose work areas have grown. The trail has become "highly controversial and volatile"[106] in New England. In such work environments, the trail is not viewed as a privilege, but the various agencies continue to follow the congressional mandate. Complete trail protection now nears 93%, and in over 1,700 land acquisition transactions, less than five percent have been adversarial. The protection parties include the UPS, the USFS, states crossed by the trail, local governments, trail clubs, and supportive landowners. This provides a fair amount of legal clout.

Neighbors are urged to become active partners in the management of the trail itself, which has proven to be cost-effective and "philosophically appropriate."[107] With thousands of volunteers and workers, including landowners, the project has become "more than just the body of land it traverses…but a resource with a soul as well as a body."[108] Much responsibility has been shifted to the ATC, which has done well in shouldering it, moving

---

[106] Pamela Underhill

[107] Pamela Underhill

[108] Pamela Underhill

from independent trail managers to "responsive community-linked managers."[109]

As a long ribbon, the trail is more vulnerable to incursions and external threats than other large projects, since the ratio of boundary to acreage is so high. There is "no core or central zone to which one can retreat."[110] A three-mile buffer is too expensive for purchase, but member awareness has been helpful. Land through which the trail passes is under constant pressure from developers, and landowners participate in litigation. Requests for power, communication lines, gas lines, and roads are an ever-present reality, Officials concede that the Appalachian Trail cannot be "The Great China Wall of the east coast."[111] More often than not, the answer lies in integration rather than through division, and much innovative cooperation has been successfully designed. Through this sensitive work, MacKaye's metropolitan to indigenous relationship continues to thrive.

Online Resources

Other 20th century American history titles by Charles River Editors

---

[109] Pamela Underhill

[110] Pamela Underhill

[111] Pamela Underhill

Further Reading

Appalachian Trail Conservancy –
www.appalachiantrail.org/explore/explore-by-state/

Appalachian Trail Conservancy, Welcome to
Massachusetts –
www.appalachiantrail.org/explore/explore-by-
state/massachusetts/

Appalachian Trail in Georgia, US Department of
Agriculture, National Forest Service –
www.fs.usda.gov/recrea/conf/recarea?recrea=62815

Appalachian Trail, Maryland Park Service, Department
of Natural Resources –
www.dnr.maryland.gov/publiclands/Pages/at.aspx

Appalachian Trail Conservancy, Welcome to Maryland –
www.apptrail.org/explore/expore-by-state/maryland/

Appalachian Trail Conservancy, Welcome to North
Carolina – www.appalachiantrail.org/explore/explore-by-
state/north-carolina/

Appalachian Trail Conservancy, Welcome to Tennessee
– www.appalachiantrail.org/explore/explore-by-
state/tennessee/

Appalachian Trail Conservancy, Welcome to Virginia –
www.appalachiantrail.org/explore/explore-by-

state/virginia/

Appalachian Trail Histories, Myron Avery – www.appalachiantrailhistory.org/exhibits/builders/mavery

Appalachian Trail, New York – www.appalachiantrail.org/explore/explore-by-state/new-york/

Asheville Trails, Appalachian trail in North Carolina – www.ashevilletrails.com/appalachian-trail-north-carolina/

Avery, Myron, H., The Appalachian Trail, *Scientific American*, Vol. 153, No. 1 (July 1935)

Blue Ridge Outdoors, 10 Stunning Viewpoints Along the Appalachian Trail – www.blueridgeoutdoors.com/go-outside/10-viewpoints-along-appalachian-trail

Comey, Arthur C., The Appalachian Trail Conference, *Landscape Architecture Magazine*, Vol. 15 No.3 (April 1925)

Connecticut Forest & Park Association, Appalachian Trail – www.ctwoodlands.org/blue-blazed-hiking-trails/appalachian-trail

Dartmouth Outdoors, About the Dartmouth Outing Club – www.outdoors.dartmouth/doc/

Foresta, Ronald, Transformation of the Appalachian

Trail, *Geographical Review*, Vol. 77 No. 1 (January 1987)

Herzog, Mary Jean Ronan, Including Appalachian Stereotype in Multicultural Education: An Analysis of Bill Bryson's A Walk in the Woods, *Journal of Appalachian Studies* Vol. 5 No. 1 (Spring 1999)

Inscoe, John, University of Georgia, Appalachian Trail, New Georgia Encyclopedia, 10/22/2002 – www.georgiaencyclopedia.org/articles/sports-outdoor-recreation/appalachian-trail

Lanza, Michael, Backpacker, Outside, July 4, 2021 – www.backpacker.com/trips/long-trail's/appalachian-trail/american-classic-hiking-the-appalachian-trail/

MacKaye, The Appalachian Trail: A Guide to the Study of Nature, *The Scientific Monthly*, Vol. 34 No. 4 (April, 1932)

Miller, D. Jason, Back-Packed Architecture: The Appalachian Trail and its "Primitive Huts", *Journal of Appalachian Studies* Vol. 21 No. 2 (Fall, 2015)

Mittlefehldt, Sarah, The People's Path: Conflict and Cooperation in the Acquisition of the Appalachian Trail, *Environmental History* Vol. 15 No. 4 (October, 2010)

NPS, National Park Service, Appalachian Scenic Trail – www.nps.gov/appa/planyourvisit/safety.htm

Nynjtc.org, Summer 2021 Walk is Here –
www.nynjtc.org

Ny-NJ Trail Conference, Welcome to the New York-New Jersey Trail Conference – www.nynjtc.org

Schaffer, Dennis, Connecting Humans and Nature: The Appalachian Landscape Conservation Initiative, *The George Wright Forum*, Vol. 133 No. 2 (2016)

Supreme Court of the United States, U.S. Forest Service v. Cowpasture River Preservation Association, Court of Appeals for the Fourth Circuit - www.supremecourt.gov/opinions/19pdf/18-1354_igdj.pdf

Trailheads, Hiking the Appalachian Trail. The Complete Guide for Beginners in 2021 – www.trailheads.com/blog/appalachian-trail-complete-guide

The Green Mountain Club, Long Trail, 1910 – www.greenmountainclub.org/about/thegreenmountainclub/

The Trek, Appalachian Trail State by State Highlights, Massachusetts – www.thetrek.co/appalachian-trail-state-by-state-profile-massachusetts/

Underhill, Pamela The Appalachian National Scenic Trail: A Neverending Story, *The George Wright Forum*,

Vol. 6 No. 2 (1989) George Wright Society

Vitali, Jacob, Appalachian Trail Proponent, Late Shirley Resident to be Focus of Historical Program, August 4, 2021, Nashoba Valley Voice – www.noshabavalleyvoice.com/2021/08/14/appalachian-trail-proponent-late-shirley-resident-to-be-focus-of-historical-program/

Free Books by Charles River Editors

We have brand new titles available for free most days of the week. To see which of our titles are currently free, click on this link.

Discounted Books by Charles River Editors

We have titles at a discount price of just 99 cents every day. To see which of our titles are currently 99 cents, click on this link.